Aston's vERy CuRIous DAY!

Written by

Catherine Wilkinson

Illustrated by

Angela Mingledorff

ISBN: 1466253657
ISBN-13: 978-1466253650

DEDICATION

Dedicated to my little man.

ABOUT THIS BOOK

These books are designed to be interesting for your child. I hope that they will find it interesting to learn about the different emotions and things that they can see in their world. With these books and also the SELIA Kids program, my aim is to promote an introduction to emotional, cognitive and environmental awareness. Research has shown that a foundation in awareness can lead to better choices, decision making and problem solving. And that these can lead to a more fulfilling life for the individual and the people around them. Part of the importance of learning these skills is the practice of slowing down to become aware of and acknowledge what is happening around us.

Often so much is happening in our lives and our children's lives that children can get over stimulated and overly involved in the situation without realising. The danger in this is that behaviours can happen that are not healthy, or sometimes not how we would usually have liked to have behaved ourselves or have had our children behave. When we become over stimulated and bombarded with information, be it social, environmental, relational, or emotional, we start to lose the opportunity to think and make decisions.

Critically we lose the opportunity to learn the skills we need to live healthy and fulfilling lives. Often we don't realise we do not have the right skills to use within the challenging situation until we really need them! This is exactly what these series of books are designed to do, to teach your child and open the communication lines to develop strong social and emotional skills. Skills such as resilience, confidence, teamwork, leadership, self discipline, delayed gratification, and emotional regulation.

You will find as you spend time with your child with these books, and implementing the techniques, that your relationship with your child will change. You will notice your own understanding is improved, your child is more responsive, and your relationship will be strengthened. The questions within the books are designed to promote conversation in general, but also to set a precedent of your child feeling comfortable in talking with you about their feelings from a very early stage where your relationship is the most important one in their life. Please use the questions as a prompt, though expand and add your own experiences to connect with your child where possible. I hope that you will enjoy them too!

Catherine Wilkinson

BA (Psych)(Hons), Dip Prof Couns, Cert Frontline Management, Cert 1 Trainer, ...and Mum!

Enjoy!

When Aston woke up this morning, he looked out the window. The sun was shining, and he could tell it was going to be a day of adventure!

I wonder what he can see...

Aston was feeling very curious. You can tell he was feeling curious because his eyes were wide and shiny, his mouth was long and thin, and curvy just on the edges.

Can you see how he looks curious today? Point to the facial features.

He was looking all around his house wondering about all the things he could see. There were so many interesting things today!

What do you think Aston is looking at? What can you see?

Yes! He was curious Alright! First, he was curious about what he could find in his bedroom. He started looking through the toybox to see what he could find. He dug his head in deep to look all the way to the bottom.

What toys can you see?

Curious about what he can see.

Then Aston was curious about what he could find outside. He saw some ants on the path. They were all walking in a straight line right across the middle.

Curious about what he can discover.

How many ants can you see?

Later on he was curious about how fast he could push his scooter around the yard.
Whoosh!
Around he goes!

Curious about what his movement.

Do you think he is going fast or slow?
How can you tell?

When Aston read his books, he was curious about all the pictures he could see.

What do you think Aston is looking at?

And he was curious about what sound he could make with the pots and pans. Bang! Bang! Bang! He drummed away!

What kind of sound do you like to make with your instruments?

Curious about what he can hear.

Mum was curious about what Aston was doing. "What are are you doing there Aston?" she asked. "Just looking", he replied with a smile.

Have you ever felt curious just like Aston? What was happening?

Later that night, Aston laid in bed and remembered all the curious things he did on his adventure day.

What can you remember he did?

Curious about what he can remember.

SELIA KIDS PROGRAM

SELIA Kids is a division of the Social and Emotional Learning Institute Australia (SELIA). It is an opportunity for parents and carers to connect with their children and teach them the vital skills they need whilst growing in these critical stages of development and especially towards starting school. Skills for development that they will carry through into adolescence and adulthood.

The Social and Emotional Learning Institute Australia (SELIA) was founded to establish social and emotional learning (SEL) as a fundamental part of child education. We operate a multi faceted approach working with families with children from 0 to 6 years through our **SELIA Kids** program, and working with principals and leaders from primary schools throughout Australia. Our consultants and program developers work with advisors in the United States, the UK and New Zealand to ensure up to date and established SEL practices.

SELIA is *Putting the Pieces Together* for child academic, social, and emotional education.

Social and emotional learning (SEL) is a strategy for developing the essential life skills necessary for greater success throughout all the different aspects of life. SEL builds the skills we all need to manage our lives, our relationships, and our study or work, more effectively and with greater satisfaction. Skills such as recognising and managing our emotions, making responsible decisions, handling challenging situations constructively, and establishing fulfilling relationships.

In respect of children, these skills help them to understand what they are feeling and make appropriate behaviour response choices that further help them to keep themselves safe and resolve conflicts or confrontations more effectively.

The Collaborative for Social and Emotional Learning (CASEL) has identified five core groups of social and emotional competencies:

·   *Self-awareness*—accurately assessing one's feelings, interests, values, and strengths; maintaining a well-grounded sense of self-confidence

·   *Self-management*—regulating one's emotions to handle stress, control impulses, and persevere in overcoming obstacles; setting and monitoring progress toward personal and academic goals; expressing emotions appropriately

·   *Social awareness*—being able to take the perspective of and empathize with others; recognizing and appreciating individual and group similarities and differences; recognizing and using family, school, and community resources

·   *Relationship skills*—establishing and maintaining healthy and rewarding relationships based on cooperation; resisting inappropriate social pressure; preventing, managing, and resolving interpersonal conflict; seeking help when needed

·   *Responsible decision-making*—making decisions based on consideration of ethical standards, safety concerns, appropriate social norms, respect for others, and likely consequences of various actions; applying decision-making skills to academic and social situations; contributing to the well-being of one's school and community

Please visit our website at www.seliakids.com.au

or for primary school educators www.selinstituteaustralia.com.au

All Titles in the Series:

Elle Doesn't Want to Play
Aston's Building Blocks
The Circus
The Surprise Gift
Aston's Very Curious Day!

www.ingramcontent.com/pod-product-compliance
Lightning Source LLC
Chambersburg PA
CBHW060808290526

45792CB00005BA/1573